Following Directions

Around the House

ISBN #1-56175-206-1

Written by Sylvia Houy
Illustrations by Eleanor Villalpando
Cover art by Danny Beck

©Remedia Publications 1990. All rights reserved. Printed in the United States of America. The purchase of this book entitles the individual teacher to reproduce copies for classroom use only. The reproduction of any part for an entire school or school system or for commercial use is strictly prohibited.

REMEDIA PUBLICATIONS   10135 E. VIA LINDA, #D124   SCOTTSDALE, AZ 85258
Toll Free 1-800-826-4740   FAX 602-661-9901

To the Teacher

The purpose of this fun-to-use book is to provide students an opportunity to practice following instructions while learning directions (north, south, northeast, southeast, etc.) and position in space concepts (around, in front of, across, between, behind, etc.).

Since the tasks can be varied and are increasingly detailed, the book may be used with a range of ability levels.

Some of the skills addressed in this book include: comprehension, thinking, fine-motor, eye-hand, visual perception, and creativity, to name a few.

The book includes:

1. **FIVE DIFFERENT FLOOR PLANS**: living room, playroom, kitchen, bedroom, and entire house.

2. **FURNITURE PIECES FOR EACH ROOM.** It is important to note that the furniture pieces appear as if one is looking down on the room. A discussion of perspective may be necessary before students begin the tasks. An explanation of symbols used on the floor plans (doors, doorways, and windows) may be helpful, also.

3. **DIRECTION PAGES FOR EACH FLOOR PLAN.** Only by following all directions on a page (e.g., Living Room 1A, 1B, 1C, 1D) will the result be a completely furnished room.

— Suggestions for Use —

This book is easily adaptable to use as a learning center.

- **CUT AND PASTE.** Provide student with a copy of a blank room floor plan, furniture pieces for that room, and directions for furniture placement. Student reads each direction, then colors and cuts out each furniture piece (not necessary to make an exact cut around each furniture piece since the floor is white and excess paper will not show), applies paste, and places it in the correct location. It is very important to mention the necessity of "planning ahead," i.e., arrange all furniture pieces in the room first before applying paste.

- **DRAWING (instead of Cut and Paste).** Provide student with a copy of a blank room floor plan, furniture pieces, and directions. Student reads the directions, then draws the furniture in the correct locations in the room. Student then colors each piece per the directions.

- **PLACE AND MARK.** For those students who find drawing and cutting difficult, it is suggested that the teacher cut out the furniture pieces and provide a blank room floor plan. The student merely manipulates the pieces and could put a color mark near the furniture piece to indicate the correct color. The teacher could also cut out and laminate furniture pieces and floor plans.

- **BE CREATIVE.** Have students design their own plans. They will enjoy creating original furniture placements and color schemes. Have them then write directions to match the plans and exchange directions with other students.

  Create other room floor plans — family room, laundry room, garage, etc.

  Enlarge the floor plans (draw on butcher paper) and furniture pieces (use enlargement capability of copy machine) for those students who find manipulating the small pieces difficult.

  Read the directions for placing the furniture to the students. Use as a listening-for-directions activity.

  USE YOUR IMAGINATION AND INVENT STILL MORE USES FOR THIS NOVEL BOOK!

Name _____

Living Room Floor Plan

1

Living Room Symbols

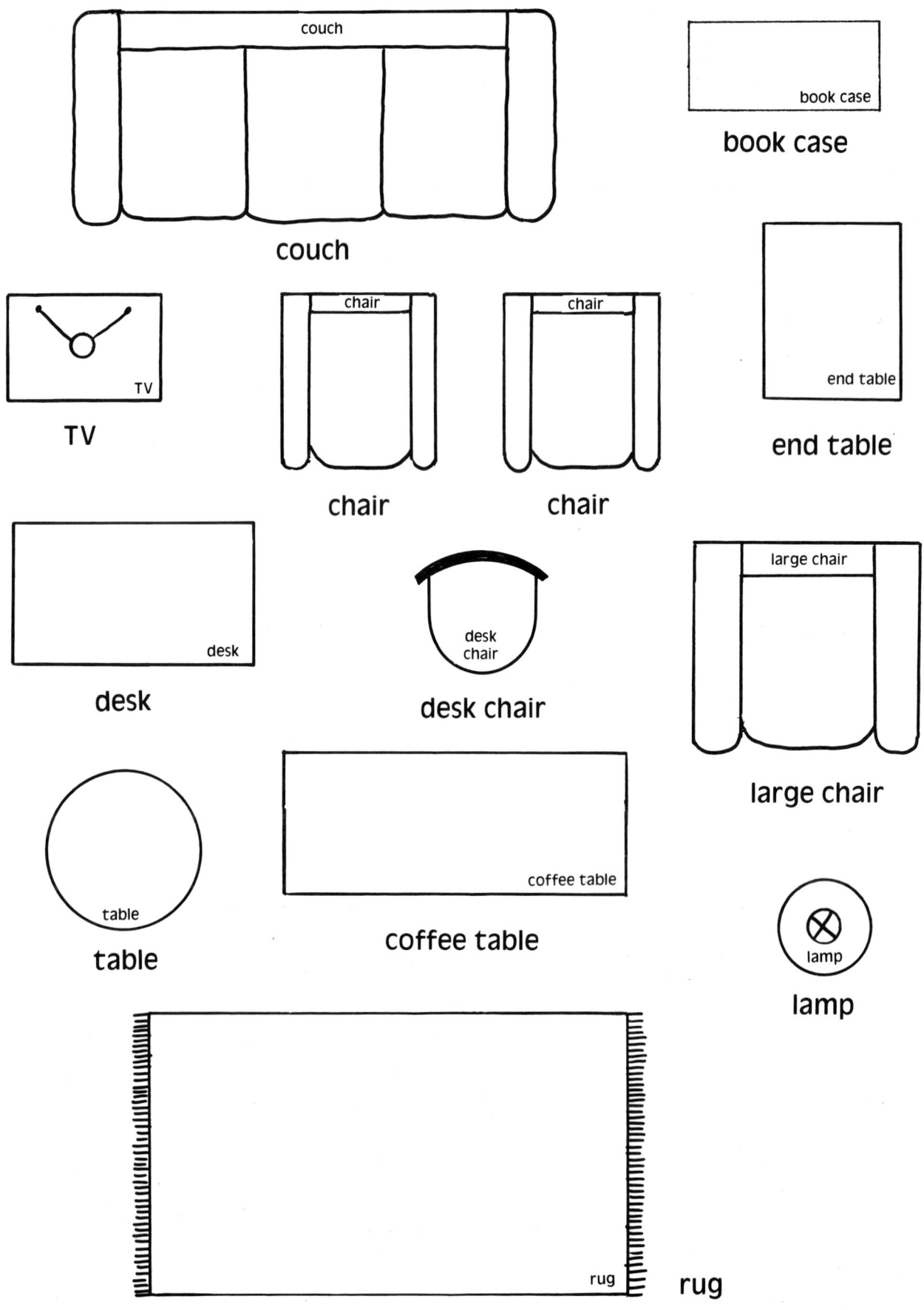

Living Room

Living Room 1A

1. Put a couch on the north wall.
2. Color the couch red.
3. Put a coffee table in front of the couch.
4. Color the coffee table brown.

Living Room 1B

1. Put the large chair north of the doorway on the west wall.
2. Color the large chair blue and yellow.
3. Put the round table next to the large chair.
4. Color the round table brown.

Living Room 1C

1. Put a rug in the middle of the room.
2. Draw a large square in the center of the rug.
3. Draw a stripe on each end of the rug.
4. Color the rug red, yellow, and blue.

Living Room 1D

1. Put the TV between the windows on the east wall.
2. Color the TV yellow.
3. Put the bookcase in front of the south window.
4. Color the bookcase purple.

Living Room

Living Room 2A

1. Put a couch in front of the windows on the east wall.
2. Color the couch blue.
3. Put a rug in front of the couch.
4. Color the rug red with blue fringe.
5. Put a coffee table on the rug.
6. Color the coffee table blue.

Living Room 2B

1. Put a small chair on the north wall.
2. Color the chair red.
3. Put a lamp just west of the small chair.
4. Color the lamp yellow.
5. Put a second small chair west of the lamp.
6. Color the chair green.

Living Room 2C

1. Put a round table in the northeast corner.
2. Draw a book on the round table.
3. Color the book brown.
4. Color the table red.
5. Put a desk in the southwest corner.
6. Color the desk yellow.

Living Room 2D

1. Put a TV on the south wall.
2. Color the TV brown.
3. Put a desk chair near the TV.
4. Color the chair green.
5. Put a large chair on the west wall.
6. Color the chair blue with green stripes.

© 1990 REMEDIA PUBLICATIONS

Living Room 3A

1. Put a rug in the middle of the room.
2. Draw a large circle in each corner of the rug.
3. Draw a large triangle in the middle of the rug.
4. Color the rug blue, green, and yellow with red fringe.
5. Put a TV on the north wall near the northeast corner.
6. Color the TV brown with a black antenna.
7. Put a large chair in the northwest corner.
8. Color the chair red and yellow.

Living Room 3B

1. Put an end table just north of the doorway on the west wall.
2. Draw a book on the end table.
3. Color the book blue.
4. Color the end table brown.
5. Put a small chair just south of the doorway on the west wall.
6. Color the chair green.
7. Put a lamp in the southeast corner of the room.
8. Color the lamp pink.

Living Room 3C

1. Put a couch on the south wall.
2. Draw a pillow on the couch.
3. Color the pillow green.
4. Color the couch blue.
5. Put a coffee table in front of the couch.
6. Color the coffee table purple.
7. Put a desk in front of a window on the east wall.
8. Color the desk orange.

Living Room 4A

1. Put a couch on the north wall.
2. Draw a pillow on each end of the couch.
3. Color the pillows red.
4. Color the couch orange.
5. Put an end table just east of the couch.
6. Put a lamp on the end table.
7. Color the lamp pink.
8. Color the end table purple.
9. Put a bookcase near the end table.
10. Color the bookcase yellow.
11. Put a TV on the west wall just north of the door.
12. Color the TV brown.

Living Room 4B

1. Put a rug in the middle of the room.
2. Color the rug yellow with red stripes.
3. Put a coffee table just north of the rug.
4. Color the coffee table brown.
5. Put a large chair in the center of the east wall.
6. Color the large chair purple and pink.
7. Put a round table near the large chair.
8. Color the table yellow.
9. Put a desk and a desk chair in front of the south window.
10. Color the desk and chair green.
11. Put a small chair south of the doorway on the west wall.
12. Color the small chair pink.
13. Put a second small chair in the northwest corner facing southeast.
14. Color the small chair blue.

Name _____

Playroom Floor Plan

Playroom Symbols

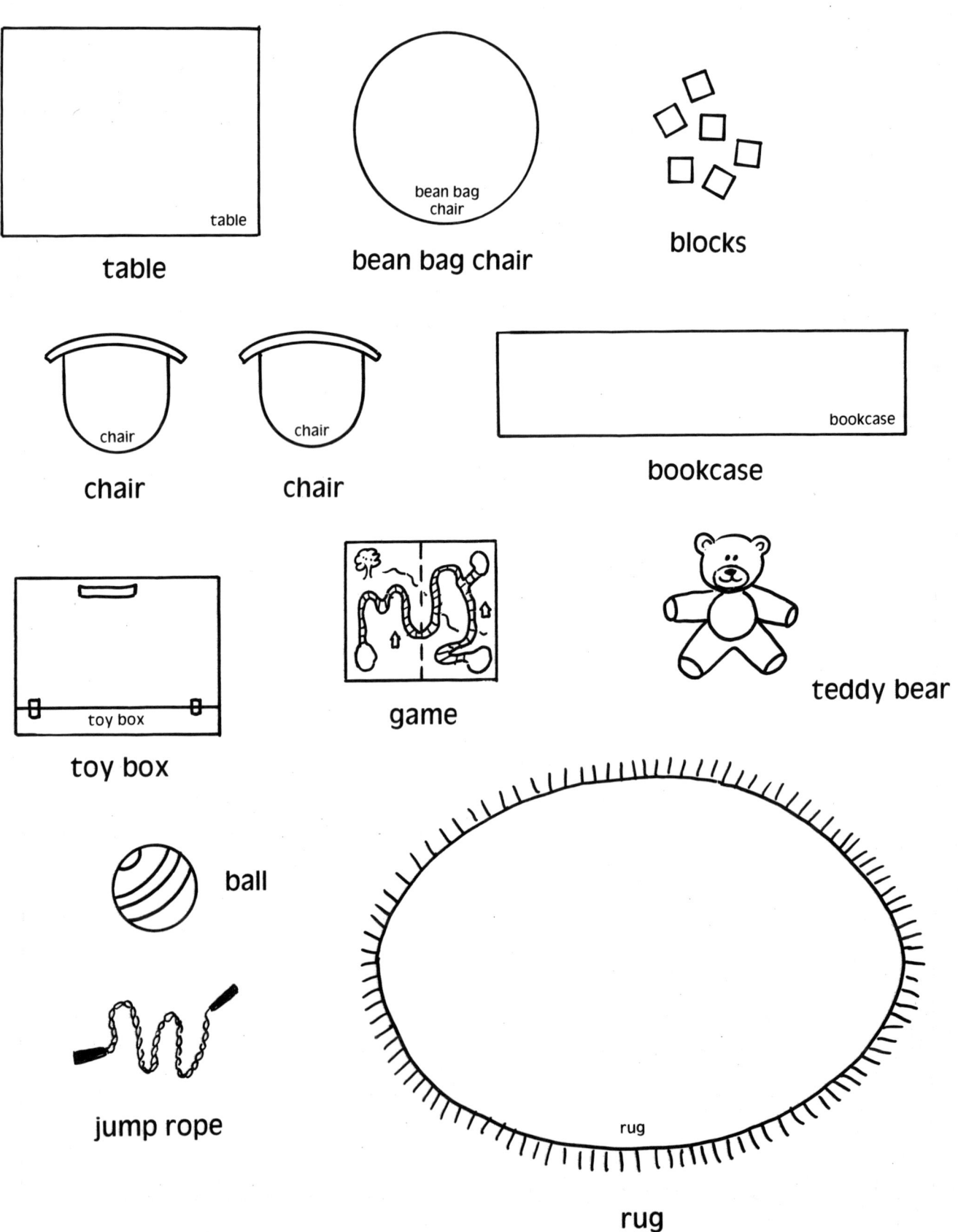

Playroom

Playroom 1A

1. Put a table on the west wall.
2. Color the table red.
3. Put a rug in the middle of the room.
4. Color the rug yellow and the fringe purple.

Playroom 1B

1. Put a bookcase under the window on the south wall.
2. Color the bookcase brown.
3. Put a ball just east of the bookcase.
4. Color the ball red and blue.

Playroom 1C

1. Put a bean bag chair west of the door.
2. Color the bean bag chair green.
3. Put a teddy bear next to the bean bag chair.
4. Color the teddy bear brown.

Playroom 1D

1. Put a toy box on the east wall.
2. Color the toy box orange.
3. Put three blocks in front of the toy box.
4. Color the blocks purple.

Playroom

Playroom 2A

1. Put a rug in the center of the room.
2. Put a teddy bear on the rug.
3. Put six blocks near the bear.
4. Color the teddy bear orange.
5. Color four blocks red and two blocks blue.
6. Color the rug green.

Playroom 2B

1. Put a toy box on the north wall.
2. Color the toy box yellow.
3. Put a chair next to the toy box.
4. Color the chair brown.
5. Put a table in the southwest corner of the room.
6. Color the table pink.

Playroom 2C

1. Put a bookcase under the window on the east wall.
2. Put a jump rope in front of the bookcase.
3. Put a chair near the bookcase.
4. Color the chair yellow.
5. Color the jump rope red.
6. Color the bookcase orange.

Playroom 2D

1. Put a ball behind the door.
2. Color the ball red and yellow.
3. Put a bean bag chair on the west wall.
4. Color the bean bag chair blue.
5. Put a game board next to the bean bag chair.
6. Color the game board purple.

Playroom

Playroom 3A

1. Put a rug in the northwest corner of the room.
2. Put four stripes on the rug.
3. Color the rug red, blue, green, and yellow.
4. Put a table in front of the south window.
5. Color the table green.
6. Put a chair just west of the table.
7. Color the chair yellow.
8. Put a game board in the center of the room. Color it.

Playroom 3B

1. Put a toy box in the southeast corner of the room.
2. Color the toy box blue.
3. Put a teddy bear on the floor in front of the toy box.
4. Color the teddy bear brown and black.
5. Put a bookcase on the wall across from the west wall.
6. Color the bookcase orange.
7. Put a ball between the toy box and the bookcase.
8. Color the ball red.

Playroom 3C

1. Put a bean bag chair on the west wall.
2. Color the bean bag chair red.
3. Put 6 blocks near the bean bag chair.
4. Color four blocks red.
5. Color two blocks yellow.
6. Put a chair in the northeast corner.
7. Color the chair purple.
8. Put a red jump rope near the chair.

Playroom

Playroom 4A

1. Put a table on the wall across from the south wall.
2. Draw a notebook and pencil on the table.
3. Color the pencil yellow.
4. Color the table red.
5. Put a teddy bear on the floor just west of the table.
6. Color the teddy bear light brown with black ears.
7. Put a ball near the table.
8. Color the ball pink and purple.
9. Put a toy box in the southeast corner.
10. Color the toy box red and yellow.
11. Put a rug in the middle of the room.
12. Color the rug purple with yellow fringe.

Playroom 4B

1. Put a bookcase on the west wall.
2. Color the bookcase green.
3. Put a game board in front of the bookcase.
4. Color the game board blue and orange.
5. Put a bean bag chair on the east wall.
6. Color the bean bag chair orange.
7. Put a jump rope next to the bean bag chair.
8. Color the jump rope purple.
9. Put six blocks south of the bookcase.
10. Color 2 blocks yellow.
11. Color 4 blocks brown.
12. Put two chairs under the south window.
13. Color the chairs blue.

Name _____

Kitchen Floor Plan

Kitchen Symbols

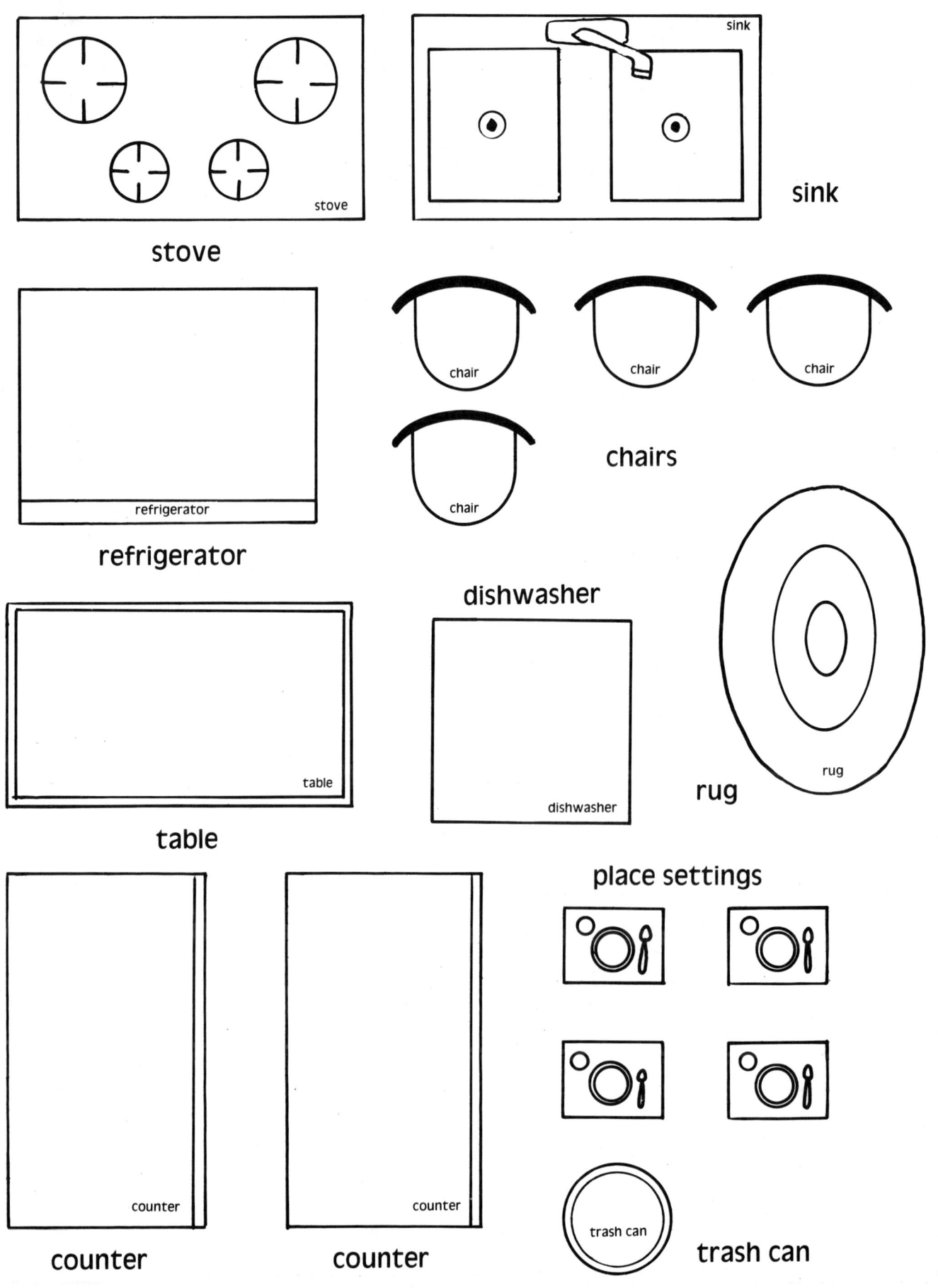

Kitchen

Kitchen 1A

1. Put a sink under the south window.
2. Color the sink yellow.
3. Put a rug in front of the sink.
4. Color the rug orange and yellow.

Kitchen 1B

1. Put a stove in the center of the east wall.
2. Color the stove brown and black.
3. Put a refrigerator on the south wall.
4. Color the refrigerator pink.

Kitchen 1C

1. Put a dishwasher in the southeast corner.
2. Color the dishwasher green.
3. Put a counter on the east wall.
4. Color the counter purple.

Kitchen 1D

1. Put a table in the middle of the room.
2. Color the table blue.
3. Put four chairs around the table.
4. Color the chairs red.

Kitchen

Kitchen 2A

1. Put a table in the center of the west wall.
2. Color the table red.
3. Put three chairs around the table.
4. Color the chairs blue.
5. Put two place settings on the table.
6. Color the plates blue.

Kitchen 2B

1. Put a sink in the center of the east wall.
2. Draw a pan in the sink.
3. Color the pan black.
4. Color the sink green.
5. Put a dishwasher just south of the sink.
6. Color the dishwasher yellow.

Kitchen 2C

1. Put a counter in the northeast corner.
2. Draw a loaf of brown bread on the counter.
3. Color the counter pink.
4. Put a stove just east of the door.
5. Draw a black pan on the right back burner.
6. Color the stove yellow.

Kitchen 2D

1. Put a refrigerator just west of the window on the south wall.
2. Draw a red book on top of the refrigerator.
3. Color the refrigerator yellow.
4. Put a green trash can in the southeast corner.
5. Put a rug just east of the center of the room.
6. Color the rug red and blue.

Kitchen 3A

1. Put a table in the middle of the room.
2. Color the table green.
3. Put four place settings on the table.
4. Color two plates blue.
5. Color two plates purple.
6. Color the spoons pink.
7. Put four chairs around the table.
8. Color the chairs orange.

Kitchen 3B

1. Put a sink in front of the south window.
2. Color the sink orange.
3. Put a counter just west of the sink.
4. Color the counter brown.
5. Put a rug in front of the counter.
6. Color the rug green and purple.
7. Put a dishwasher next to the sink.
8. Color the dishwasher blue.

Kitchen 3C

1. Put a refrigerator in the northeast corner.
2. Color the refrigerator yellow.
3. Put a stove on the east wall.
4. Color the stove brown.
5. Put a counter on the west wall just north of the window.
6. Color the counter blue.
7. Put a trash can near the stove.
8. Color the trash can blue.

Kitchen 4A

1. Put a table in the center of the south wall.
2. Color the table pink.
3. Put three place settings on the table.
4. Color the plates red.
5. Color the spoons purple.
6. Color the glasses yellow.
7. Put three chairs around the table.
8. Color two chairs brown.
9. Color one chair black.
10. Put a trash can in the southeast corner.
11. Draw two red boxes in the trash can.
12. Color the trash can blue.

Kitchen 4B

1. Put a stove in the northeast corner.
2. Color the stove yellow.
3. Put a counter next to the stove.
4. Color the counter brown.
5. Put a refrigerator near the stove.
6. Color the refrigerator blue.
7. Put a sink under the west window.
8. Color the sink green.
9. Put a dishwasher just south of the sink.
10. Color the dishwasher brown.
11. Put a counter just north of the sink.
12. Color the counter blue.
13. Put a rug near the sink.
14. Color the rug red and yellow.

Name _____

Bedroom Floor Plan

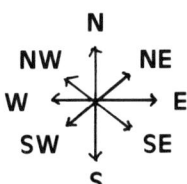

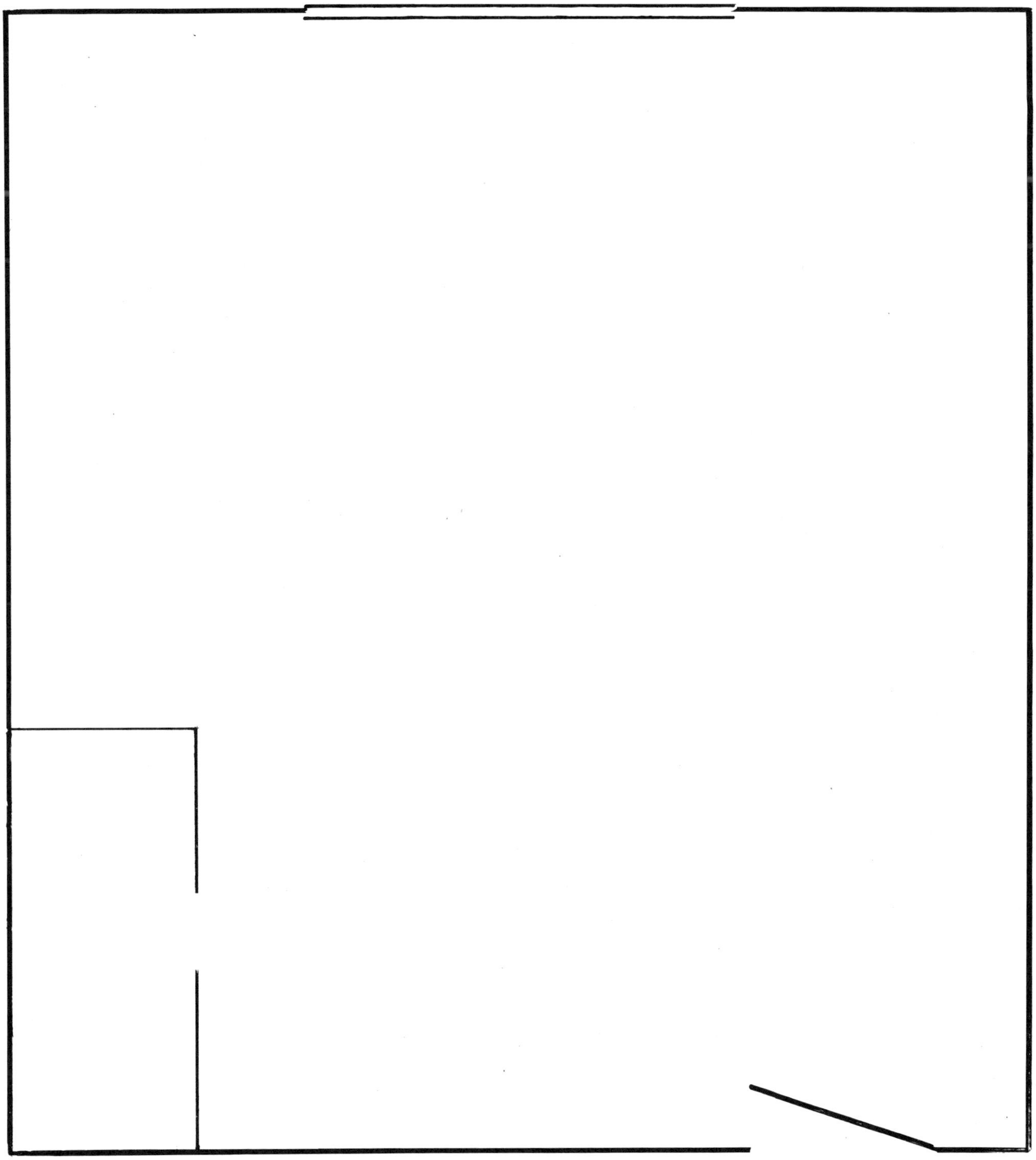

Bedroom Symbols

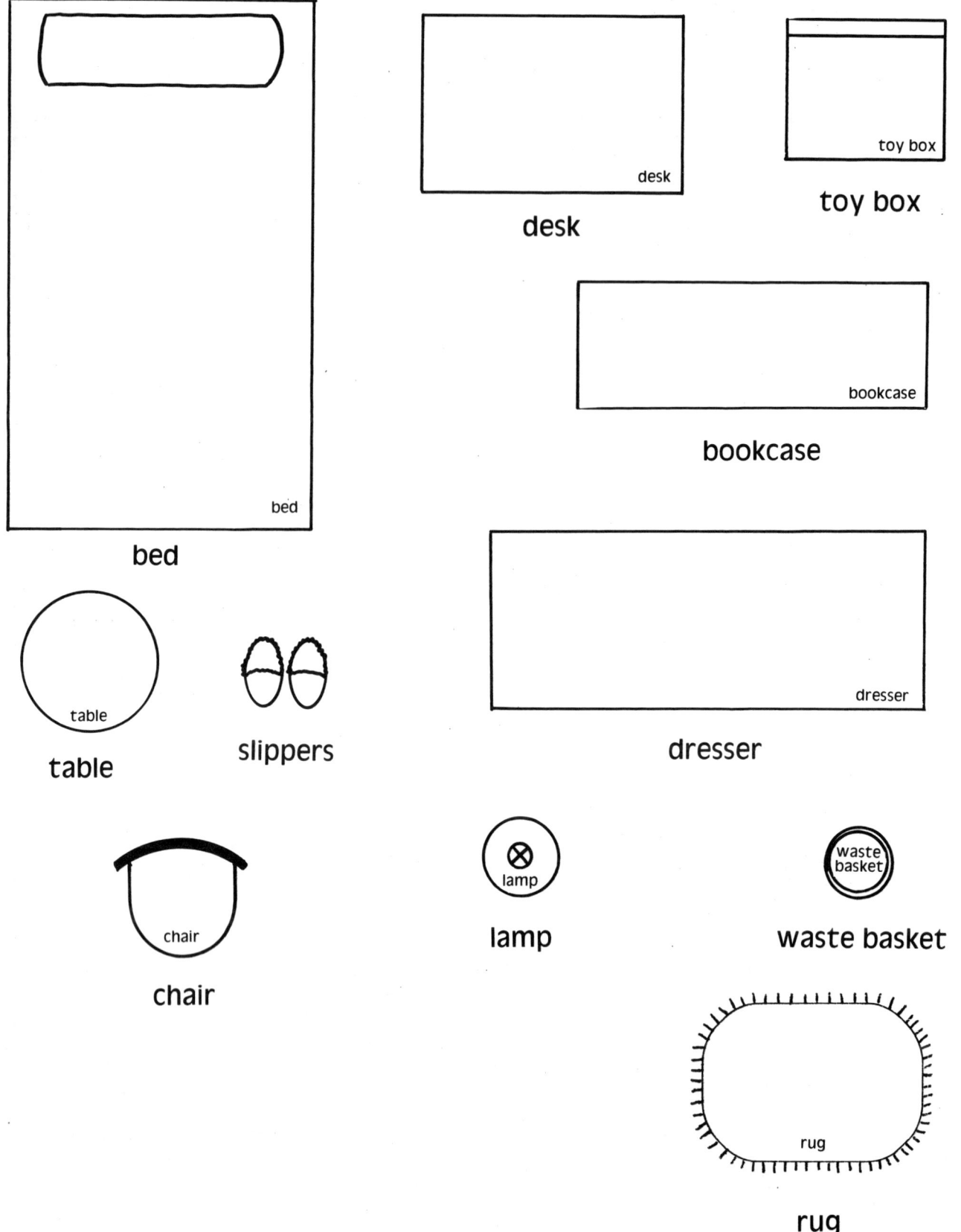

Bedroom

Bedroom 1A

1. Put a bed on the east wall. Place the head of the bed against the wall.//
2. Color the bed blue.
3. Put a table just north of the bed.
4. Color the table brown.

Bedroom 1B

1. Put a pair of slippers in the closet.
2. Color the slippers red.
3. Put a pink dresser on the west wall.
4. Put a green rug at the foot of the bed.

Bedroom 1C

1. Put a wastebasket on the wall behind the door.
2. Color the wastebasket red.
3. Put a bookcase under the window.
4. Color the bookcase red.

Bedroom 1D

1. Put a desk just west of the door.
2. Color the desk purple.
3. Put a lamp in the center of the desk.
4. Color the lamp pink.

© 1990 REMEDIA PUBLICATIONS

Bedroom

Bedroom 2A

1. Put a bed under the window. Place the head of the bed under the window.
2. Color the bed pink.
3. Put a pair of slippers on the left side of the bed.
4. Color the slippers purple.
5. Put a dresser on the west wall.
6. Color the dresser blue.

Bedroom 2B

1. Put a toy box in the northwest corner.
2. Color the toy box red.
3. Put a table on the east side of the bed.
4. Color the table yellow.
5. Put a lamp on the table.
6. Color the lamp pink.

Bedroom 2C

1. Put a wastebasket in the closet.
2. Color the wastebasket yellow.
3. Put a rug in front of the door.
4. Draw and color flowers on the rug.
5. Color the rug blue with green fringe.

Bedroom 2D

1. Put a bookcase on the south wall.
2. Color the bookcase pink.
3. Put a desk on the east wall.
4. Color the desk blue.
5. Put a chair near the desk.
6. Color the chair yellow.

Bedroom 3A

1. Put a bed against the east wall.
2. Color the bed green.
3. Put a chair in the northwest corner of the room.
4. Color the chair red.
5. Put a rug in front of the chair.
6. Put a large circle in the middle of the rug.
7. Color the rug blue and yellow.
8. Put a blue wastebasket in the southeast corner of the room.

Bedroom 3B

1. Put a table under the window.
2. Color the table purple.
3. Put a lamp on the table.
4. Color the lamp pink.
5. Put a pair of slippers next to the table.
6. Color the slippers orange.
7. Put a toy box in the closet.
8. Color the toy box red.

Bedroom 3C

1. Put a bookcase just west of the door.
2. Color half of the bookcase red.
3. Color half of the bookcase blue.
4. Put a desk just north of the closet.
5. Draw a pencil on the desk.
6. Color the pencil yellow.
7. Draw a red notebook on the desk.
8. Color the desk purple.

© 1990 REMEDIA PUBLICATIONS

Bedroom 4A

1. Put a bed in the center of the east wall. Put the head of the bed against the wall.
2. Draw polka dots on the bed.
3. Color the bed blue and green.
4. Put a rug on the south side of the bed.
5. Color the rug green with yellow fringe.
6. Put a table on the north side of the bed.
7. Put a lamp on the table.
8. Color the lamp orange.
9. Color the table yellow.
10. Put a pair of slippers on the rug.
11. Color the slippers red.
12. Put a chair in the closet.
13. Color the chair green.

Bedroom 4B

1. Put a dresser on the west wall.
2. Draw a comb and brush on the dresser.
3. Color the comb and brush yellow.
4. Color the dresser green.
5. Put a toy box in the northwest corner.
6. Color the toy box pink.
7. Put a red wastebasket in the closet.
8. Put a bookcase just west of the door.
9. Draw a red book on top of the bookcase.
10. Color the bookcase purple.
11. Put a desk under the window.
12. Color the desk blue.

Name _____

House Floor Plan

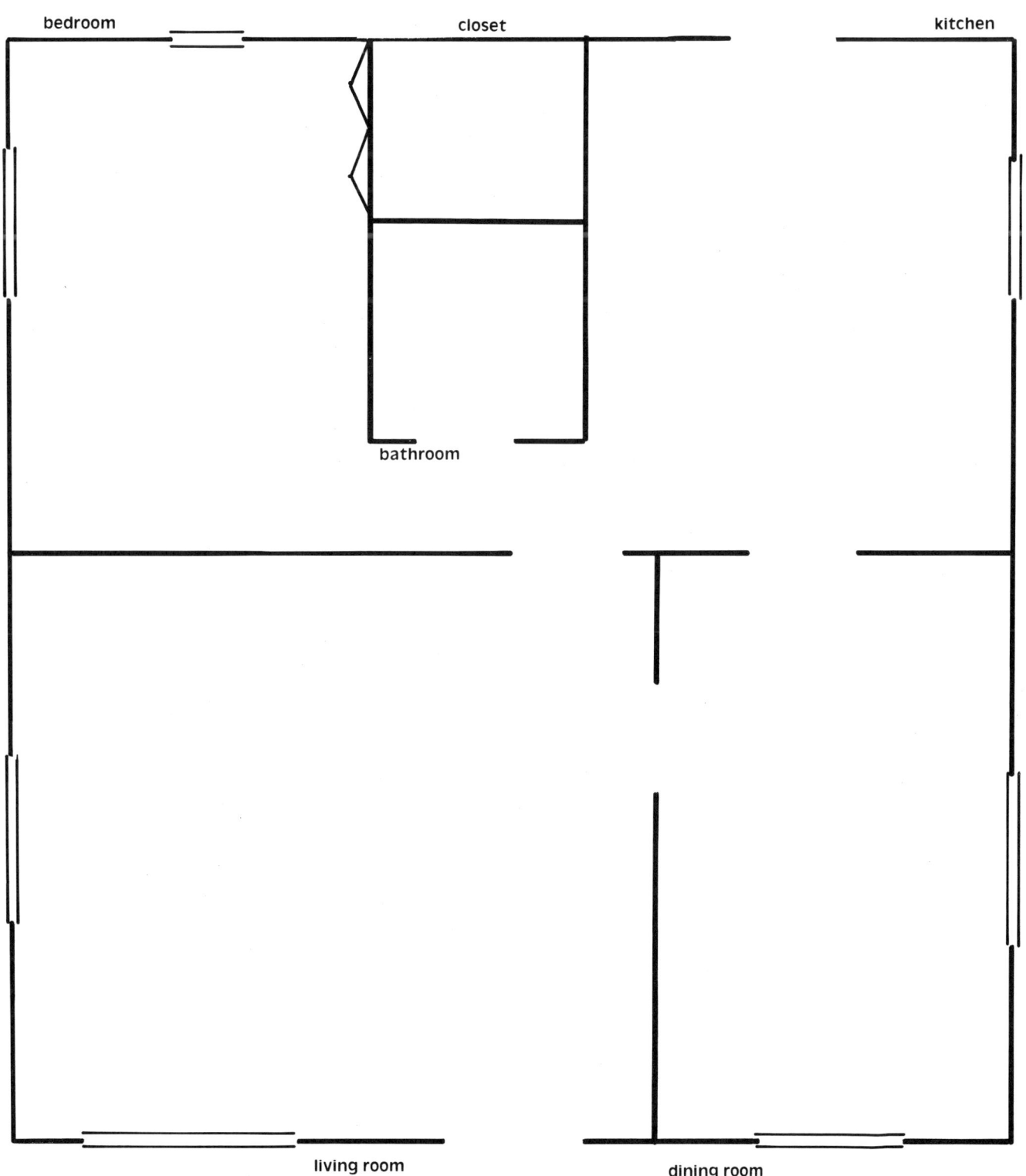

© 1990 REMEDIA PUBLICATIONS

House Symbols

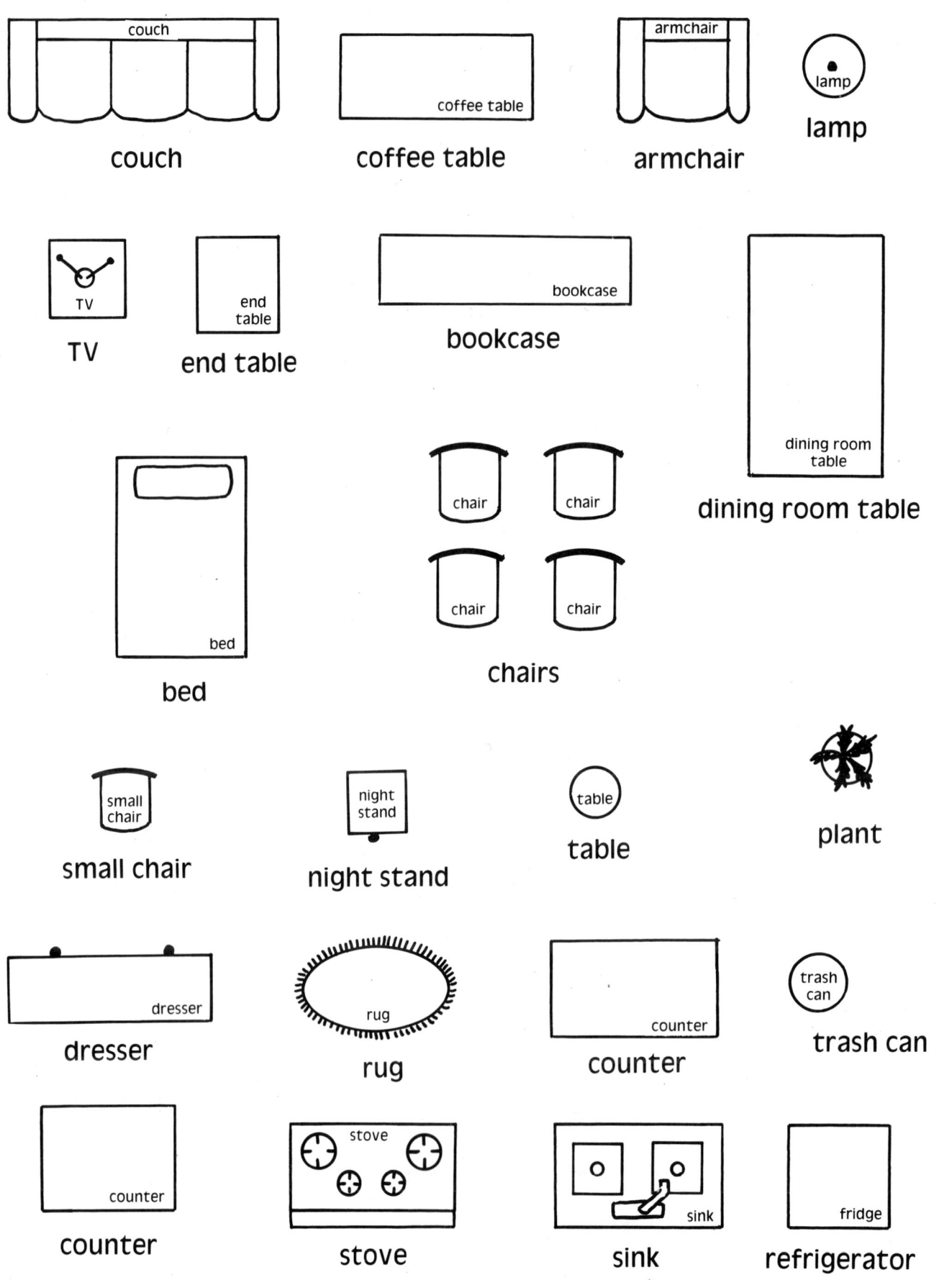

26
© 1990 REMEDIA PUBLICATIONS

House

House 1A

1. Put a couch on the west wall of the living room.

2. Color the couch red.

3. Put an armchair just east of the window on the south wall of the living room.

4. Color the armchair blue and red.

House 1B

1. Put a stove on the south end of the west wall of the kitchen.

2. Color the stove yellow with black burners.

3. Put a counter next to the stove.

4. Color the counter blue.

House 1C

1. Put a bed under the west window in the bedroom.

2. Color the bed pink with red polka dots.

3. Put a dresser in the center of the bedroom's south wall.

4. Color the dresser brown.

House 1D

1. Put a table in the center of the dining room.

2. Color the table brown.

3. Put four chairs around the table.

4. Color the chairs purple.

House

House 2A

1. Put a couch on the north wall of the living room.
2. Color the couch blue with green stripes.
3. Put a coffee table in front of the couch.
4. Color the coffee table brown.
5. Put an armchair just south of the window on the west wall.
6. Color the armchair purple.

House 2B

1. Put a dining room table in the center of the dining room.
2. Color the table orange.
3. Put four chairs around the table.
4. Color the chairs yellow.
5. Put a plant in the southeast corner of the dining room.
6. Color the plant green.

House 2C

1. Put a bed under the north window in the bedroom.
2. Color the bed blue and red.
3. Put a night stand next to the bed on the left side.
4. Color the night stand purple.
5. Put a dresser across from the bed.
6. Color the dresser yellow.

House 2D

1. Put a sink under the window in the kitchen.
2. Color the sink green.
3. Put a refrigerator in the northeast corner.
4. Color the refrigerator yellow.
5. Put a stove across from the sink.
6. Color the stove brown and black.

House 3A

1. Put a blue couch in the center of the living room facing north.
2. Put a red rug in front of the couch.
3. Put a purple armchair in the center of the north wall in the living room.
4. Put a brown end table on the right side of the armchair.
5. Put a yellow lamp on the end table.
6. Put a yellow bookcase just behind the couch.
7. Put a green plant in the northwest corner of the living room.
8. Put a brown coffee table just south of the door on the east wall.

House 3B

1. Put a yellow sink under the window in the kitchen.
2. Put a blue refrigerator in the northeast corner.
3. Put a yellow counter next to the sink.
4. Put a blue stove across from the refrigerator.
5. Put a yellow counter next to the stove.
6. Put a red trash can just west of the doorway on the south wall.
7. Put a pink dining room table in the center of the dining room.
8. Put four red chairs around the table.

House 3C

1. Put a green bed on the south wall of the bedroom.
2. Put a yellow night stand next to the bed.
3. Put an orange dresser on the north wall.
4. Put a brown TV on the dresser.
5. Put a small, blue chair just south of the closet door.
6. Put a red, round table next to the chair.
7. Draw a bathtub, sink, and toilet in the bathroom. Color them.
8. Draw a pair of black shoes in the closet.

© 1990 REMEDIA PUBLICATIONS

House 4A

1. Put a red and pink couch in front of the west window in the living room.
2. Put a brown end table in the northwest corner of the living room.
3. Put a pink lamp on the end table.
4. Put a red armchair in the center of the north wall of the living room.
5. Put a brown coffee table in front of the couch.
6. Put a yellow, round table next to the armchair.
7. Put a green bookcase under the south window of the living room.
8. Put a brown TV just south of the doorway on the east wall of the living room.
9. Put a purple dining room table in the center of the dining room.
10. Put four pink chairs around the dining room table.
11. Put a small, orange chair in the northwest corner of the dining room.
12. Put a green plant in the southeast corner of the dining room.

House 4B

1. Put a yellow counter in the northwest corner of the kitchen.
2. Put a blue sink next to the counter.
3. Put a red and yellow rug in front of the sink.
4. Put an orange stove in the southeast corner of the kitchen.
5. Put a yellow counter next to the stove.
6. Put a green refrigerator next to the yellow counter.
7. Put a blue trash can on the south wall of the kitchen.
8. Put a purple bed under the west window in the bedroom.
9. Put a blue dresser on the south wall of the bedroom.
10. Put a pink night stand in the northwest corner of the bedroom.
11. Draw a pair of green shoes in the closet.
12. Draw a bathtub, sink, and toilet in the bathroom. Color them.